SKY RAY LOLLY

SKY RAY LOLLY

Fiona Pitt-Kethley

Chatto *&* Windus

LONDON

Published in 1986 by
Chatto & Windus Ltd
40 William IV Street, London WC2N 4DF

Second impression

British Library Cataloguing in Publication Data

Pitt-Kethley, Fiona
Sky ray lolly.
I. Title
821'.914   PR6066.15/
ISBN 0-7011-3046-6

Photoset by
Rowland Phototypesetting Ltd
Bury St Edmunds, Suffolk
Printed by
Redwood Burn Ltd
Trowbridge, Wiltshire

Contents

ACKNOWLEDGEMENTS

Some of the poems first appeared in the following:
London Review of Books, Poetry South East 8, Spare Rib, London Reviews
and *New Statesman*; one was broadcast on Australian Broadcasting
Corporation Radio Two.

Sky Ray Lolly

A toddler on a day out in Herne Bay,
on seeing an ancient, civil-servant-type,
I held my Sky Ray lolly – red, yellow
and green striped, pointed, dripping down between
my legs and walked bandy. My Ma and Pa,
(old-fashioned innocents like Rupert Bear's),
just didn't notice this and ambled on,
that is, until they saw the old man's face,
jaw dislocated in surprise. They grabbed
that Martian's willy from my little hand.

The world still sees me as a nasty kid
usurping maleness. A foul brat to be
smacked down by figures of authority.
All things most natural in men, in me
are vice – having no urge to cook or clean,
lacking maternal instincts.

And they would take my pride, my rocket
of ambition, amputate my fun and geld
my laughter, depriving me of colour.
And smirk to see my little lolly melt,
me left with a stick.

Tragedy

My father, a Philistine journalist,
(as his father and grandfather were before),
took me to see *Romeo and Juliet*.
'What a shame about that nice young couple,'
he said. 'Why *did* they have to die!'

Tragedy's quite addictive in its way —
the irritation keeps you reading on.
I went through Hardy at an early age
hoping to find one book at least where things
weren't buggered up for all the characters.
Heroes and heroines are not ill-starred —
they're just dishonest, never talk things out —
that's all.

'But don't you realise,' I told my Dad,
(I was a cynical fourteen), 'that pair'd
have bred. There'd be a million fools by now,
all horribly romantic as the first,
all trying to spoil their own or others' lives.'

'I think they should have changed the end' he said,
'for modern audiences.'

Bums

My Head, Miss Harold, five foot square in grey,
was deeply disappointed that the shrink
she had me sent to certified me sane.
(At seven, I'd written 'BUM' upon my desk,
and that, in Old Harry's view meant madness.)
'They pluck these words' she said, 'out of the air!'
(That was the only time she didn't use
'If however . . . ' her Johnsonian catchphrase.)
'Perhaps,' my mother said, 'she got it from
A Midsummer Night's Dream?' The Head just blinked.
What had she missed? The school editions were
all bowdlerised. My mother was quite wrong.
I'd only read Hamlet – no comedies –
and that play does not, as I remember,
have a bum, or even the ghost of one.
Like any normal child, I'd plucked, (Miss H.
was right), that word out of the air while I
was playing Bums – a game where little girls
(or boys) compare size, shape and texture bared.
Ma should have known – she once caught three of us,
standing, minus our navy knickers
in a front-room window, near the piano.
(I don't remember if we planned to play.)
Startled we saw a white face staring in
between the pink hydrangeas and the road.

Hate at First Sight

Soldiers, a TV documentary said,
could volunteer as subjects for a course
of mental torture. They just endure it
for extra pay or leave. Nothing was told
of fighting back or keeping self-respect.

The first few years at school I learnt nothing –
their books and spelling were too simple,
the paints too thin. My first true lesson
came at nine.

Before, I'd felt little resentment
and shrugged off being labelled daft or deaf,
never needing to cry in front of them.
Then, some kid put another's handwork down
the loo and I was blamed.

I'd been brought up on heroic stories
which said if you looked people in the eye
and told the truth you'd be believed at once.
It doesn't work.

Our form-teacher in her twin-set and pearls
was round-faced and always smiling
as the Iron Maiden of Nuremberg.
Each day I met the furnace of her hate.
She'd call me out of class, interrogate,
then send me back in tears – or I'd break down
and cry, then be sent out – to her.

Years later, when I tried to talk of this,
I saw my hands begin to shake, jerking
the coffee from my cup. I had to stop.

Trapped in a vacuum of despair, that term,
I thought dramatically of suicide,
but lacked the means. For weeks, bound by my school's
strict etiquette, I simply parried blows.
I lost all sense of time. Day after day
my head and eyes ached too much to learn.
I sat bowed in my desk, too numb to hate
her back as she tried to put the class against me,
threatening to keep them in as well, if I
did not confess.

Deep inside, when my last tear was strained out,
I found the truth.

Teachers and Fate give some a Captain's badge,
drop others in the shit. There's no reason,
no help to be had in a cause like that.
Fighting's the only dignity that counts.
One by one, I won my classmates over,
convinced my enemies as well as friends.

First Love

The object of my love sat halfway down
the church — tall, fair and almost twice my age.
A hardened choirgirl, I had all by heart,
and watched him through the seasons of the year
in anthems, collects, choral eucharists.

On weekdays I would cycle by his home
and stand up on the pedals as I passed
to see the garden he was never in.
And if the curtains stirred, I'd race around
the block, then slowly ride by once again.

At home, I only hinted that I thought
he looked like a Greek God. 'Bit weedy, though!'
my mother said. I bored my friends. One pinned
a note upon his gate — our names linked with
a heart — 'Is it requited?' underneath.

His mother, meaning to be tactful, took
that letter to the vicar, who burnt it
in a bizarre ritual. 'That girl ought to
be shot!' he said — I think he meant my friend —
and bent to strike a match by the church door.

I didn't cycle past much after that
and kept my eyes on psalters and hymn-books.
I still enjoyed singing 'Love Divine' though,
and I still kept on making Freudian slips —
'Lead us into temptation' being my best.

I peeped from behind prayer-folded hands
as I knelt, thinking it a subtle ruse,
I also got the odd look processing down
the aisle behind 'Old Humpy' with his cross,
my Scholls clacking on the heating-gratings.

I started to pose a little, wearing
blue eyeshadow to match my cassock and
lilac on my bare toe-nails, (cheap offers from
some magazine), trying not to notice
another figure sitting in his pew.

When I'd convinced myself that girl whose hand
he held must be a relative, the banns
were called. I hid my sorrow in a sneeze.
Back home, hysterical, I screamed, 'Only
four years to wait and I'd have been sixteen.'

A Sunday Afternoon

Seeking adventures one church-free Sunday,
I crossed the Dives-Lazarus divide
from Ealing into Acton on the bike
I had for winning a free place at ten,
and chained it up to Springfield Gardens' gate.
It was your average London park, complete
with flasher, park-keeper, geraniums,
a bum-splintering see-saw and baby swings.
I soon got talking, and a girl of seven
was pointed out, who always dressed in pink
and used to suck men's willies in the Gents.
I thought it seemed a funny thing to do.

The boys didn't use the swings or see-saw,
but stood a little way off, watching us,
hands in pockets. An Indian twelve-year-old
crossed the gulf, sniggering, and asked if he
could 'plant his carrot in my turnip field'.

Soon, we were rescued from moral danger;
the 'Firebrands' evangelists descended
asking the question 'Are you saved?' We weren't
too sure, and so they kidnapped and bussed us
to Acton's Co-op Hall for Sunday School.
A gaggle of children, matted or plaited,
our hands reeking of the metal swing-chains,
we were ready to try anything once
and sang 'I will make you fishers of men',
even the little cocksucker in pink.

Taking Off

Sometimes, spontaneously, a group of girls
gathered in the playground. Half a dozen
or more pairs stood, grasping each others' wrists.
No-one ever really suggested it
and we never knew the name of the game.

When your turn came round you'd take off and dive,
landing on a mattress of arms to be
tossed several times before their holds slackened
and you slid down twisting on to the grass.
With your eyes shut you felt you were flying.
I could never understand why Tom Brown
didn't enjoy being tossed in a blanket,
except, tastes differ.

That game was considered too physical.
Like leapfrog and friendships with older girls
the teachers always put a stop to it.

The Staff Room had a squarish bay-window
which looked out on the grass where we played.
Daily one hot summer, two girls lay there
in each others' arms, kissing, mouths open,
a button or two of their turquoise blouses
left casually undone, their hands straying
occasionally inside – blatant – you'd think
they'd have saved it for some empty classroom
separating quickly if a prefect
came through the door.

The grass they always lay on parched yellow.
Daily we waited for the skies to fall.
The Head would delegate the job, we thought,
and send a minion to prise them apart.
There were various legends extant about

people who'd been expelled for cannabis,
abortions and calling the English teacher
a cow, (brave on a quart of Woodpecker).
That pair obviously just had it coming.

One day, after Prayers, as we sat cross-legged
on the parquet listening to notices,
in a round about sort of way the Head
gave out she'd seen something that might upset
the people in a block of flats nearby
and give a wrong impression of the school.
We pricked up our ears. 'Some of you,' she said,
'have been taking off your white ankle socks
in public, on the grass.'

The Party

On my tenth birthday I had a really
dirty party – whoopee cushions, the lot.
The respectable list of games my Ma'd
planned were all despised. When eating-time came,
we renamed everything, sickening ourselves –
turds on sticks, bum sandwiches – and we shook
up the jellies like bosoms. Afterwards –
Pin the Pants on the Headmistress,
Truth or Dare and Dirty Consequences.
During Forfeits, we had a girl stripped down
to her red Ladybird tights. My mother came
to the rescue – not that my friend was pleased –
there had been a prize of threepence riding
on her silence. (We've kept in touch since school.
Some years back, on a train to Pitlochry,
she had the Canadian Ice Hockey team
for three quid – she's always been a sports fan.)
One Judas girl of the twelve sat silent –
like Queen Victoria, not amused – and went
rather early. The rest, combed and bourgeoised,
left with their parents, saying as usual,
'Thank you for having me.'

10 SYLL

Ghost Stories

'Don't peep or the Bogey Man will get you!'
my great grandmother'd say as she held kids
under her shawl, but I looked in vain from
my mother's cardigan and no-one came.

At school, I told others ghost stories –
but could feel no frisson of fear myself –
James, Poe, Le Fanu, with added horrors.
'Have you heard the one' I'd start over lunch
'about the rotting nun?'

There were two odd handles in the front rooms
of our Victorian house. One was painted
pale grey like the Study's walls, the other –
brass-plated wearing thin. 'Some sort of bell
to call servants in the old days.'

When I was on my own I'd take a breath
and slowly move one of the handles up,
imagine *them*, turning the knob softly,
opening the door and coming in.

I'd visualise a pair – maid and butler
perhaps, in black going a little green,
their hair and eyebrows white, aged farcically
beyond old age, like the oldest members
of dynasties in epic film sagas.

Then, I'd put the handle back down again
and make them go away.

Pigeons

I used to love to watch their delicate
shades of grey as they swaggered on the lawn,
jostling for bits of bread I'd left for them.
I'd lean on the chipped chocolate brown sill
and name them to myself as Arthur's knights –
the same set came there every day – Gawain,
Lancelot, Perceval and Galahad,
a white one – Guinevere.

I made my parents tell me bird stories –
'Belinda the demon pigeon of Acton
lived above a gargoyle in a graveyard . . .'
reassured by the repetition
before reading widened my choice. I searched
upstairs, (my father'd cooed realistically
and thought of bringing a clay pigeon home
to plant on the mahogany wardrobes,
just peeping down, but out of reach.) One day,
in the way that stories sometimes come true,
a grounded pigeon hobbled through the door.
We kept her in a box in a back room.
Close up, I decided, birds weren't so nice.
She pecked our hands for food and glared at us
with her red eyes. I never liked her much.
The room began to smell of feathers and shit.
She took a lover too – a ponce of a pigeon –
we nicknamed him Albert, I don't know why.
He would puff out his petrol-shaded chest,
come in through the open window, rape her,
knock her about a bit, then steal her seed.
That was if the cat didn't tumble her first.

The vet just broke her neck. 'The best way,' he said,
standing there, the limp bird in his hands.
'She wouldn't have flown again.' My father

came home angry, buried her box and all,
calling him a wretched amateur.

If I pass the dirty-grey wallowing mass
in Trafalgar Square and hear the rattle
of seed in tins I remember Lucy
and feel disgust, some fear perhaps – not quite
a phobia – disgust at her cold end
before my father's eyes, fear at her role
of victim, a lot which could be anyone's.

'The Mirror Crack'd'

It was days of filming in the warm sun –
a stately home in Kent – the grass was shorn short
under small fruit trees, the green broken with
heraldic bursts of red clover, self-heal
and yellow bird's foot trefoil. Some cows
looked on across a fence.

One time the locals descended, spoiling
shot after shot, standing in the foreground
in their non-Fifties polyester frocks,
before they got down to the autographs.

'Please sign my book for me, Miss Taylor.'
Five minutes later they were round again.
'Can't remember if I asked you,' one woman said.
'I've just done Angela Lansbury. If not,
please sign.'

The woman called her husband up to look.
'Ooh, isn't she beautiful?' They peered closely.
She sat motionless on a wooden bench,
her violet chiffon dress caught on splinters.

The man stood thinking. His belly peeped
from a small tear in his orange nylon shirt
close by her face. 'Nah!' he said. 'Take off
all that powder and paint and she'd be just
like you or me.' He rammed his cap down hard
on his oiled hair and went off comforted.

Wankers

I once went to an art film festival.
The first film was composed of lengthy shots
of ploughing, Yoga, wanking, intercut.
You'd see a strip or two being ploughed, followed
by the film-maker's seedy little wife,
pompously and unseductively nude,
piously tying her legs into a knot.
The slob was on next, pulling at himself.
(A friend had held the camera for that bit.)
The thing went on for half an hour at least.
I thought of going for a coffee, but,
at last, the grand dénouement came – sperm hit
the mirror at his feet – a teaspoonful.
I felt like shouting 'Who's a clever boy?' –
he'd tried so bloody hard. But he was there,
with all his family, enjoying *his* film.

The Old Vic's *Spring Awakening*'s borstal scene
contained a masturbation comp. (One night,
one of them came on stage – he'd probably done
it for a bet.) I got my Ma a seat.
She didn't like the play. But going home,
we spotted one of those actor-wankers –
he looked the sort she'd label nice young man –
reading a Penguin Classic on the train.

Cherry Trees

The specious charm of cherry trees with their
drain-clogging, Andrex-coloured blossoming
leaves me unmoved. I can't say that I blame
George Washington, or, my father who
nobbled our London one by pruning it.
The week-long shower drives me up ladders
to shift the putrid, pink confetti-gunge
that stops the gutters up. Although I take
a saw to our St Leonards one, break down
branches and make spitting fires from them,
the thing just grows and burgeons horribly,
poking its voyeuristic tips against
our neighbour's place. They're easy-going, but . . .
I was quite glad when Polly, next-door's cat,
(a ginger-mutant-she from Dungeness),
ran up and piddled through our bannisters
from three floors up, down on my fresh-washed hair –
it gave me something every bit as bad
as that foul tree, for a complaint if I
should need one – there were witnesses.

I wish I had just half the strength of those
who handled scenery at the Old Vic –
superbly philistine, they saw each play
in terms of overtime, and Chekhov as
'A load of bloody cherry trees to shift!'

Merging

In *Dogs of War* a Cockney extra gave me
some good tips for survival.

'Never put yourself forward –' he advised,
'we're in it just to be anonymous –
the more so, the better.' He'd merged enough,
he said, to fill the place of umpteen men
on the Titanic's decks. 'Crew, passengers,
waiters – the ruddy lot!' Eventually,
some young assistant sussed him out and pulled
him from behind the bar, saying: 'I never want
to see that ugly mug of yours again.'

'Just mingle, join any queue you see –
it's probably for grub . . .' – not quite such good
advice. Getting in line, I thought for tea,
I nearly got myself stuck with a beard
in *Reds*. His mingling, on the other hand,
brought him an extra day in some beer ad.
They left him gilded in an anteroom,
(one rower too many for the quinqereme),
to mind the others' clothes – he only had
a loincloth on – forgotten, sweating gold,
alone.

I've seen him since, I think, merging in films,
tucked away, round the corner from a set
in Pinewood, selling watches from a case.
I saw his brawny arm at Shepperton
amongst an octopus of hands stealing
the cream cakes from a tray while other men
confused the cook with change. And he was
one of six who leaned the table down,
left three accountants grovelling on the ground
for cash and chits, and took us into more
paid overtime.

Night London

The pubs were out, the evening's takings done,
box-office hatches tightly closed. The girls
and boys of Theatre-land waited for their
release, hustling their patrons to the Strand.
'All out?' the firemen asked, huge padlocks
in their hands. The day's last workers left
by stage doors set in alleyways.
The night began . . .

A steel-blue lightness in the half-dark
of the Charing Cross Road marked the Classic's foyer —
all-night horror and coffee — three fifty.
The Chinese usher handed little packs
of sickly shortbread buttons to the queue,
then disappeared behind a hatch to dole
out plastic cups of coffee — frothy pale —
sugar and milk compulsory. Two films
and a reel on in the musty dimness
a ticketless straggler wove the side aisle;
bottles dropped from his sodden carrier-bag.
The balding plush soaked Cyprus sherry up.
A policeman, manoeuvring, got him
by the intact elbow of his pee-stained mac.
The emergency exit's long bolt scraped
on concrete. Lamplight flooded in.

The river wind chilled the brightness of squares
and bridges, lifting the sick garbage smells
from stores and restaurants, drying the grimed dew
of parks and monuments. Next day's papers
lay in the great old stations, fresh with print.
Outside, the streets were bare, light, free,
the Tubes all latticed shut.

Lying

One of the sex manuals we swapped at school
decreed the husband should not kiss his wife
in the final stages. The theory was
that women choose to fantasise about
some handsome star and not the bloke they're with.
His face too near to theirs might bring them back
to grim reality and thus prevent
orgasm.

Their men are vibrators with pay cheques,
brainless, feelingless fucking-posts, engines.
These dutiful wives will stoke their boilers,
fill their tanks to keep them running. Then,
they're faithful in their fashion to Paul Newman
when the lights go out and the lying begins.

It seems OK to want to shut *pain* out.
When I was tipped back in the dentist's chair
I sent myself to a Baroque theatre
amongst gold, white and blue decorations
to the music of Mozart, as his drill
screamed clumsily on a back tooth. It would
seem positively perverse to savour
moments like that and feel them as they are.
But *pleasure*? How can they close off like this,
never experiencing the nuances
of individual feeling and technique –
not seeing the only point of being there
was wanting each other more than the rest
for that short time – lying till sex becomes
duty, a daily pinta, Sunday joint
or yearly jab?

One wife I knew fancied Stewart Granger,
forever 'Scaramouche' buckling a swash.
(Do older ones think necrophiliacly
of Douglas Fairbanks Senior and John Gilbert?)
Her husband, she said, still didn't love her
in spite of her 'bat's hole'. (She'd had their kids
by Caesarian to keep it small.) At night,
he'd lie crying to himself and wanking,
muttering some other woman's name.

The Fear of Splitting Up

I've always had a horror of the splits,
though flexible enough in other ways —
the lotus is no problem and I can sing
and drink water, standing on my head.

Though I'd not advocate a lifestyle where
my legs were never the least bit apart —
the fear of splitting up will always stop
me half a dozen inches from the ground.

I could just see myself like some old peg,
a scissors that has lost its middle screw,
or Mistress Jekyll and old Mother Hyde —
two halves apart leading their different lives.

Sex Objects

I learned from a friend's porno mag that men
can buy the better class of plastic doll,
(posh ones are hard and unyielding, not the
pneumatic sort that fly from windows when
they're pricked), in slow instalments, torso first.

Well-qualified in wanking, Mark saves up
his pennies till they grow to pounds and then
invests in Ingrid, just the body, for
his carnal press-ups – a bit too flesh-pink
for human, and she sports a ridgy seam
where back meets front. Mark humanises her –
steals her a black lace bra that doesn't fit,
(he's not that used to seeing naked tits),
and puts a cover of a Cosmo girl
up on the pillow where his doll's neck ends.

Six months on, tired of screwing her pink trunk,
he spends his pocket money on a head –
a bald one comes by post – mouth a red O.
He buys his girl a man-made fibre wig,
and, graduating to fellation, talks
about her to his friends.

He gets the arms for Christmas and soon gives
his doll a voice – a steamy tape – he's good
at it by now, he thinks, and she should tell
him so. The tape's a great success at first,
until he starts to get the timing wrong,
and Ingrid, moaning says 'It's wonderful'
after he's gone.

Mark's not a legs-man, so these limbs come last –
a duty – something to hook round his back.
He's shocked when they arrive – one black, one white.
The firm's in liquidation and could just

[31]

supply him with the halves of two whole pairs.
(The black's from 'Sonia', another doll.)

That limb cures his Pygmalionitis quite.
He starts to look for human girls to fuck,
but finds they usually need persuasion first,
their fannies aren't so neatly set in front
and, unlike Ingrid, they can criticise.

Country Walk

I went into the countryside for a walk
and took some bread for the ducks
and my camera to take photographs.
As I carefully shut the farm gate
the old bull said 'Leave that open
Missus, I want to see that
heifer next door — last time she
had a headache.'
I went to the pond and threw bread to the ducks —
'Stuff your Mother's Pride' they said,
'We wants worms.'
I put up my camera to take a picture of a nest,
and the birds said 'God damn that voyeur,
let's crap on her lenses.'
I sat down for my picnic.
There was a little hedgehog nearby,
I undid my thermos and poured him some milk.
And the hedgehog said, 'Keep your filthy
cow-muck, I haven't got stomach ulcers.
What I want is your pin-cushion for a dildo.'

Penis-Envy

Freud, you were right! I must expose my id
And show the penis-envy that lies hid.
It's not that I admire the look as such,
It seems a strange adornment for a crutch,
Like sets of giblets from a butcher's shop,
Two kidneys with a chicken-neck on top,
Floating serene in baths like lug-worm bait,
Or, jokily bobbing with the jogger's gait.
Fig-leaves, I'm sure, are prettier far than cocks,
And only suffer greenfly not the pox.
As tools, pricks really aren't reliable,
One minute hard, the next too pliable.
If I had bought a hammer or a chisel
As changeable, I'd think it was a swizzle.

It's not that I'm against them in their place,
But simply that I cannot see a case
For cocks to be a sort of union card
In life's closed shop. I think it very hard
That humans with these fickle bits and bobs
Are given a fairer lot and better jobs.
If only I'd had one of them, it seems
I could have had success, fulfilled my dreams.
A female eunuch though, all I'll attain
Is Pyrrhic victory and trifling gain.

Red Fish

At thirteen I bought a tuppenny packet
containing two red fish with instructions
from an old shabby newsagent's in Cork,
where they sold copies of The Red Letter,
(romantic nurse and doctor stories
with Orphan Annie on the back), odd eggs,
bacon, (priced by the rasher not the pound),
and ice-white Chilly Willy lollies.

The cellophane fish curled in my hot palms –
the pack declared me 'Passionate'. Next term,
I took them into school. We used to try
sex quizzes out of mags. (You either lied
or were humiliated by lowish scores.
The ones who'd brought them in, mysteriously,
would come out tops.) My two red fish labelled
my friends 'Indifferent', 'Cold' or even 'Dead'.

At that stage, most of us tried no *real* tests.
Made cruel by religion I'd indulge
in the longest kisses and little else,
stopping myself the only way I could –
turning to rigor mortis in boys' arms –
too gauche even to say the reason why,
cold as the fish in other people's hands.

Life's harder when your body's reflexes
become the points of proof, with men
who dutifully ask you if you've come –
(why can't they tell?) – and then dispute your 'Yes'
because they think your chest's not flushed enough,
or pride themselves your nipples are erect,
forgetting that they'd left the heating off.

Apples

Where are the old apples,
the conical, uneven apples, obscurely ribbed,
ripening to deeper yellow,
the crimson-cheeked apples,
marbled and washed with clear red,
the deep lively green apples,
strewed with silvery scales, dark-spotted,
speckled like hens,
brownish, orange-tinged against the sun,
veined in grey russet, angular,
smooth-skinned,
the transparent apples grown on sand,
the Bantam's-egg-sized apples,
the child's-head-sized apples,
the red-fleshed Sops-in-Wine,
anise-flavoured New Rock Pippin,
fennel Ross Nonpareil,
Pitmaston Pine Apple, balsamic Sack and Sugar,
the strawberry and violet flavoured Calville apples,
the waxen-yellow aromatic Gravenstein,
transparent as porcelain,
pine-flavoured Lord Burghley, musky Reinette Franche,
homely Costard, Catshead, Hoary Morning,
Nanny, Cockpit, Hall Door, Bedfordshire Foundling?

On the shelves are our apples — the apples we deserve,
thin-stalked, unctuous, even green, polished to an
    inconsistency,
flesh sub-acid, cardboard-pipped, eyes stamenless,
sweating under the lights like a crowd of nervous actors.

Habeas Corpus

When the excavators had all moved out,
turning the old green of the mound
to a chequered A to Z of black-brown
earth, stringed squares populated with a sort
of house spirit, brushing and scraping
the stones, filling trays with fragments of pots,
a temporary household, together,
ministering only while time allowed,
the land gave up its expected secrets.

Several cists – coffins of stone set on edge –
revealed inhumations and cremations,
burnt-bones, frequently a blue or green tinge
due to presence of phosphate of iron,
charcoal, the remnants of a pig or goat,
a man's bones in the foetus position,
food-vessels before and behind the head,
ash-grey, marked with thong or cord impressions
and lines drawn with a pointed instrument.

The finds, scrubbed with a toothbrush, marked in ink,
catalogued for some local museum,
tell only half the story. The last cist –
flint, jet and food-vessel, but no body,
a mystery. The archaeologist explains
air or unforeseen agencies led to
the total disappearance of the bones
or else the barrow was not searched fully,
and blames the inexperienced volunteers.

A Piece of Jade

The first class in a course on Chinese Art –
we sat around, fulsomely holding forth
on tiny objects that our tutor'd brought,
all small enough to be hand held by us,
useful things, he'd said, everyday objects,
some obvious, some not, all well-crafted,
carved and polished to great smoothness.
One struck us by its simple elegance;
our Philippino lecturer looked on,
amused by our pretentiousness. (Although,
we later heard the tale of how he'd won
a grant to set up an illicit still
and urinated at a festival,
distilled it, drunk it and then peed again –
a symbol of the earth's renewal, of course –
and, if you're not too squeamish, a nice way
to earn your bread.) He soon let out, the long
and subtly-polished piece of jade I held
was an old arsehole-stopper from a corpse,
set there to keep the evil spirits out.

La Vie Bohème

Some arty type had said he wished to buy
a large Expressionistic nude I'd done,
but changed his bloody mind. So I was stuck.
Carrying canvasses is quite an art –
I held its stretcher by the middle bar,
hoping the wind wouldn't catch it like a sail.

I was pissed off enough to take a drink
off Dracula so I propped up my daub
against a café wall in the King's Road
when an old artist offered me coffee.
He gave his name and then declared with pride,
'Modigliani painted my arsehole once!'
'How come?' I said. 'Like this – when I was young
my famous uncle who adopted me
was friends with him, let him mind me one day.
He took me to the Paris Zoo. I saw
the new white rhino there and shat my pants
with fear. He brought me to his studio
and cleaned me up with a large whitewash brush.
That's how!'

He drew my portrait next – I have it still –
my face (or anyone's) surrounded by
a moon, a star, a cow, a fiddle and
a fish, all done in lilac fibre-tip,
'avec toute mon affection' scrawled beside.

Then he proposed that I should marry him,
hinting that he had plenty in the bank.
'You could just pose for me,' he said. 'I'm much
too old to do a thing. You could just lie
or stand there while I read you Robert Burns.'

Crap Literature

I have this penchant for crap literature –
a sort that's rarely kept by booksellers.
I've had finds in jumble sales and rescued
recherché items out of skips.

We think we know it all now, and banish
our far-flung ideas from this world into Space.
I like the creatively preposterous
Edwardians who had no such inhibitions
and built unique arch-villains with panache –
the *Strand Magazine*'s beautiful doctor,
one of whose crimes involved a vase breaking
on a note of a tune she had written,
Gaston Leroux's convict, Chéri-Bibi,
who swapped his face by plastic surgery,
(without an anaesthetic's aid), for that
of the fiancé of the girl he loved,
Guy Boothby's torturing Doctor Nikola,
appearing in China, Tibet, London
and Italy, burning herbal truth drugs
or killer incense in his shrine.

I love the strange interiors – not plush,
mahogany or sepia-tinted prints,
piano-legs dressed up in knicker-frills –
Le Queux's anarchist safe-houses
full of bombs, severed heads and automata,
Pemberton's island cities, copper-covered ships.

Some thrillers blind us with their science.
'The World's Finger' shows crime-solving at its best –
the victim's eyeball, properly cut out,
reveals the killer on the retina.

Others I like for their sheer messiness.
Take the example of 'The Devil's Die'.
Three men in love with the same girl. The one
who gets her then decides to bump her off
and gives her cholera, although they sleep
in the same bed. He gets it too and dies.
She cracks up. Meanwhile, in the USA,
the other two get premonitions and
turn back, lost in the Sage Brush on the way.
(The locals hadn't liked the look of them.)
Mohammed Ali, an Indian doctor,
who being coloured's not allowed to get
the girl, saves his young artist friend for her
by filling his pith-helmet with marrow cracked
from dead buffaloes' bones.

Kids . . .

I've been trying to write all this afternoon
in a large room that looks out
on the basement garden — a garden only reached
by climbing out of the middle window.
Out come 9 little bastards, staying next door —
a commercial for abortions. One has
a cap-gun, another has some arrows —
he targets a hydrangea. A whoop.
I climb out and pick up the wood arrow,
minus its red sucker, from beneath
the stone bench. Kid 3 hangs from the wrought-iron,
mouth open catching flies. 4 flips a coin
in. 5 attacks the passion-flower, uncurls
its tendrils. 2 shoots again and out I go,
nice smile, must be civilised. I hand

up the arrow. The air stinks of caps.
6, 5 and 4 start a spitting contest
into Michaelmas daisies and ferns.
The arrow's back. 2, blonde and bold,
jumps down in the rock rose, scattering pink
petals. He's hauled up by the scraped elbows,
reverse-absailing past the palm. I bite
back the shout of 'Bugger off!' turn
and try to forget – I've written in crowded trains.
Then that cunt 7 drops its dummy
in the forsythia. 8, her sister, climbs
the black railings, catching her fat teenage
bum (in its white cotton skirt) on the pink
rambler. I'm glad. 9 comes up to free her.
The dummy is retrieved from down
by the iris-roots, where the snails copulate
on a dank bed of enchanter's nightshade
and shepherd's cress, and stuck straight back
into the baby's mouth. The Rediffusion
man's drill screams through the window-frame,
brown cable snakes in through the hole.

Goat Show

The show, was due to start at two o'clock;
one judge, white-coated, entered up some names;
a tousled Toggenburg and herd looked on.
The owner, rumpled as his goat, had two
grey upright feathers in his hat, like horns.
Some half hour late, the others came along –
large spotted Anglo-Nubians, Saanens,
blow-dried white kids, another Toggenburg.
The first, bored to malevolence, shat round.
His class was next – (a second out of two).
His bloke, disconsolate, questioned the judge
and went off scratching his short beard. The rest
stood round in groups or knelt on half-bald knees
stained by the grass. The Anglo-Nubians
posed like a nest of tables by the ropes.
I sat down on the only patch of turf
left currant-free. A chocolate kid crept up,
fresh from undoing someone's Indian skirt,
and kissed me just like Andrew Marvell's nymph's
young fawn – a pleasant moment till I saw
it press its tender lips against the bold
triangularly-folded rectums of
its peers. 'She's been so good,' her mistress said.
'It's her first show.' Eight classes on, after
some small resentments, almost every goat
has a rosette – red, blue or green. Four wait
for 'Best in Show', ('Reserve Best', too,
a category that's seldom found in life).
'This year', one owner whispers gratefully,
'they didn't pick up his receding chin.'

Guide Dog

On Wednesdays in St Leonards, by the shops,
a wicked guide dog leads her master wrong.
The man is doubly blind, quite unaware
he's being kept waiting by each empty road.
'Come on,' he says to her gently, 'Come on!'
attributing the knocks and bumps he gets
to the crass carelessness of passers by.
His smiling golden retriever leads him on
through various conversing groups, then stops for fleas,
or tramps him off the kerb and into shit.
Nobody dares to interfere.

It's like some marriages – you just can't say
'That bitch has led you up the garden path!'
Some wives or husbands quite enjoy the times
their pompous partners put a foot in it.
There's not much harm in that. More sinister –
some watch like spiders for the other's end.
After my father's death, my mother found
envy, not pity, in most women's eyes.

One day, perhaps, I'll hear a screech of brakes
and see the blind man overtaken,
the hand that held her harness lightly, broken,
a day-glow band still wrapped around his arm,
the dog, a Levite, on the other side,
preening to take another owner in.

The 4.15

The 4.15 from Charing Cross, juddering
its way through Sussex, spilled my carrier-bag.
A horn of plenty on the rack, it poured
a half-erect telescopic umbrella,
some black seamed tights and jasmine tea, wet gloves,
a slow cascade of books, (mercifully
the Tampax stayed aloft). The final touch –
a box from the Loon Moon Supermarket
(sweetened kumquats) hit an old military type
in the balls. He took it well.

The four men opposite were all smiling
after my ritual of apologies.
They'd read the *Love Life* lying on the floor
as something other than a Poetry book.

Chestnuts

At Kew, the keepers let us take windfalls –
quinces, cherry apples and sweet chestnuts –
I'd feel the prickly cases through my gloves,
picking them from the muddy ground beneath tall trees.

Once we got lost there, away from the landmarks
of the Pagoda and hothouses,
and suddenly came upon the river,
saw Syon House in the distance,
serene as a steel engraving. It was
a long walk back, our winter boots clogged with
a cornflake-mass of leaves.

That evening I roasted the chestnuts I'd picked
with my friend, stripping their cases carefully.
Small, large, uneven, slightly warped – I named
them after boys I thought vaguely fanciable,
balancing them on the fire's black iron bars
till they exploded. (The first to blow
was what my friend's mother termed 'Mr Right'.)

That night I dreamt of the white marble grate.
The two Staffordshire horsemen stood guard
either side of a small lantern clock.
Time had stopped and the house had become cold.
I knelt on the carpet where I'd sat earlier,
(my face flushed then, my eyes burning and dry).
Now, the fire had gone, only ash remained.
I lifted the brass fender and got to work
pulling the crude green tiles away by hand.
Dust and cinder fragments stuck beneath my nails.
I found dead foetuses behind in rows.

Thoughts After a Burglary
For my father

In a recent break-in, some tapes of mine
were stolen, one of which contained the last
and only record of my father's voice.

He took me as a child to the sights
of London, obvious and minor, churches
of every sect, strange shops and restaurants,
tutoring me in feats of endurance –
eating the hottest Madras curries
at a tender age, swallowing a quart of pop
without taking my mouth off the bottle,
bagpipe impersonations in subways,
writing things on graffiti-proof tiling,
tearing tin cans in half and lobbing them
into the passing goods trains, and so on.

The memories are all blurred now, but there's
just enough to leave me with a strange sense
of déjà vu in any part of London.

There were once yearly parties too,
where he'd clown as Charlie Chaplin before
the little beasts from my snob school – walking
in suddenly, tripping over a raped
and ruptured, Egyptian leather pouffé
with pictures of camels and pyramids
and people all turned sideways for the tourists,
he'd somersault, (all sixteen stone of him) –
the laughter of the kids enough payment
as they sat, venomous in nylon frills.

In time, he lost his journalist's job. He'd
lived in the shadow of his successful
father – self-made, writer of ripping yarns,
fifty years editor of The Wide World.

And we got poorer in a time when dole
was not the norm. Later — a short term job —
educational précis, took him to
London's technical libraries. I went
with him in the holidays, quietly
reading odd manuals, dictionaries,
whatever was available, staring
in a trance at Adam ceilings, or out
through high windows at warehouses with doors
opening, four storeys up, on to nothing.

Then followed years, a phrenetic period of
letter-writing for jobs, the sending of
curricula vitae, getting up at
dawn, endless endless letters, and at night,
putting a slop-pail of vast and bloody lights,
(bought for our cats dirt-cheap from a friendly
butcher who enjoyed Dad's filthy jokes),
against the back-door to stop the burglars.

My father, a pensioner, at last, turned
cat-herd with some twelve furry apostles.
My parents moved out of London then,
while I was away at Art School. The thieves
my father dreaded really hit in the new place — not
clean like the London ones — these scattered papers,
tore, destroyed, dumped books out in the rain
and took almost every little thing he owned —
his bits and bobs of militaria —
all the pomposity of the Army
vanishing into a thief's pocket.

After a slow and gradual depression,
a month before my twenty-first birthday,
his heart gave out. Sensing something
I had come home a day early. We found him lying
on the lavatory floor, a livid cut

where he had struck his face in falling,
in shirt and pullover a size too small.
The undertaker took him in a pushchair
like a baby.

Some cats outlasted him and I became
their gravedigger – a new role thrust on me.
The last, a lame, alcoholic she-cat
who'd lacerated his back
into a Grünewald Crucifixion, lingered for years,
and ran to meet me every time I sang
in imitation of my father's voice.

The thieves contributed to rob me
of my ally, silencing him twice over.
What's left? A strong enduring influence –
a part of my voice that's his.

The Ecumenical Movement

My first years were haunted by foreign names,
phrases like 'apostolical succession'
and strange invasions of dressed-up prelates.
After a quick ordination, blessing
or what have you in the chapel, they'd go
out the back to take their photographs.
(I liked the geometry of our garden –
first, the square washing-line that wouldn't spin,
then the two apple trees set in the lawn
forming a triangle with the pear outside
the circle of a fairy ring.) They'd stand
there more or less, say 'cheese' in their mitres,
copes and glasses, then troop inside for tea.

I was usually bored so I'd put on
a kind of cabaret – lick out the jam
from tarts, striptease, bring in a brimming pot,
sexually harass the better-looking men –
except when some Ukrainian Count was due
and I was sent to Margate with my Mum.

My father's hobby was the marrying
of sect to sect, patching up old schisms
to make a whole and undivided church.
(He even asked Ian Paisley to join
in a wonderful stroke of naivety
or taking the piss – I've never quite known which.)

He held vast correspondences with priests,
archbishops, curés and archimandrites –
all of the smallest denominations.

The American ones gave him degrees,
the Russians magazines he couldn't read,
the Italians titles. Duc de Deauville
was the prettiest.

Our chapel was in the slope of the roof
with tatty repro-icons spaced around,
a pale oak-veneered altar touched by worm,
bottled holy water, rose oil chrysm
and souvenir crosses on the mantelpiece
above a small gas fire, and a huge loop
of light-cord trailing from a naked bulb.

My mother rarely liked my father's friends.
One of them brought his 'favourite choirboy'
to see the London sights. 'We always sleep
in separate beds,' he said defensively.
He sat there with his leg wagging
and left a little damp spot on the chair.
(We kept that seat solely for visitors
like a Siege Perilous. Eventually
we sold the dining-room set to knockers.)
Another, a most frequent visitor,
we heard had got married to a black girl
and was ashamed of her and kept her down
the basement of his Fulham house – her
and their two children. To his friends he was still
a hapless bachelor scrounging free meals.
(I spoilt that though by forging Christmas cards
to all those friends from him 'and family'.)
The last I heard he was selling hair oil
through ads on the back of a literary mag.
One man decided to christen my Dad
Mar Rupertus – 'Mar' he said, was Persian
for Lord. (He called his cat Mar Pluto too.)

I always liked my father's weird parcels –
strange stamps and seals and semi-papal bulls,
the family trees of those descended from
Avignon popes, (all covered in gold-leaf),
an altar-cloth depicting all Christ's wounds
to be embroidered in red silken thread –

a sort of kit that came with a small bone
from St Eutychius. I have it still.
I hardly like to throw the thing away.
(How hard to deal with the small useless bits
that people leave behind them when they go!
I have a superstition about waste
so bunged a contraceptive pack and odd
cigars in handbags at some jumble sale
to give their purchasers a nice surprise.)

Sometimes it was like living on the edge
of a thriller. One Frenchman wrote about
his long campaign to convert Lucifer
and told us he was getting near his aim.
Next thing we read he'd been knocked down and killed
upon some Paris street. And Mum received
a shaky note from nice old Doctor Crowe —
it must have been the last he wrote — saying
he'd give me 'lessons in magic'.

And there was the 'autonic eye' we kept
stashed in the coal cellar for years. Seemed much
the size and shape of a well-wrapped severed head,
I thought. (I used to read a lot of Poe.)
A bishop from South Africa had asked
if we would mind the thing, bribing us first
with a big box of grapes and a large tin
of chocolate fingers.

Ties

A friend picked up a couple in a club.
They took her home and tied her to the bed
with string saved from their Christmas packages.
The husband screwed her hard while his wife watched.
Her turn came next, viewed by my friend. After,
they had to cut her knots with nail scissors.

I've far less trust than her so I'd not let
myself be tied by or to anyone.
I even half resent the subtle bonds
laid on me by those men who specialise
in doing the right thing, so confident
of their technique. They play it by the book –
their book not mine.

Some people even appear to like the type,
and feel a need to sweeten things – take 'love'
in life, tooth-rotting sugar in their tea.
Caught fly-like in the treacle of romance,
they boast of gifts received. (I'd rather be
a source of schadenfreude to my friends –
tell them the tales of how a kinky Turk
gave me a woollen thermal vest to wear,
a man stuck 'jewels' he'd gathered from the beach
on to his letters with elastoplast.)

What Comes Next

A wife I'd met for the first time filled up
her used glass for me at a private view —
a tacky sort of symbolism. I saw
one of her hairs left swimming in the dregs.
As etiquette required, I pulled it out
and drank. She sat and smiled indulgently,
a broken-mirror heart on her lapel.

The second meeting I had toast from her,
burnt black as coal under lavish butter.
I ate it slowly, wondering if she'd kicked
it round the kitchen floor or spat on it,
wondering what comes next.

Audiences

The actors, standing in brightness, see just
the first few rows and scatters of faces —
Baroque angels in gilt clouds — where small lights
illuminate the Boxes or bulges
in the Upper Circle's curve.

The ushers, in the dimness, clearly see
the audiences whose tickets they have torn —
the sombre families for Ibsen plays,
sourly old and dressed in musty black,
Equus types — deep into psychology
and bent, tourists who're 'doing' the Royal Court
next week, but don't know what is on, those who
were driven to Shakespeare by exams and seem
relieved to find he's full of dirty jokes,
some who want jam on it — bums, tits *and*
culture. These last come with binoculars —
they're more high-powered than opera-glasses —
and sit in the front rows for any play
with nudity or sex.

Those who cleaned up defined the audiences
in other ways — 'a filthy lot' for more
old-fashioned plays like *Eden End* — they all
sucked sweets.

Girlie Mags

I do not care a toss if blokes must look
at glossy, big-boobed photos of bad girls.
I've met some centre-stapled, double spreads
who laughing took the cash and went their ways.
Women cannot afford to turn work down.
But how I hate the letters in those mags —
A. had her nipples pierced, linked with a chain,
B. had the firm's alsatian yet again,
C., buggered by six fellas, felt no pain,
and all loved it. So the male bastards claimed,
signing their missives with sweet female names.
All right, my guess is good as theirs, I'll write
and sign the thing John Smith. Last week I put
my bollocks through a mangle, and loved it.
May I recommend?

Swimming Baths

In Acton, the Public Baths' attendant
was not the life-guard type you might expect.
You'd see his fishy, chlorinated eyes
above the doors. He'd got it to an art —
parading past the cubicles, checking
the locks still worked, peering at ground level
for extra pairs of feet.

A serious few entered with a low dive,
thrusting forward, their heads in wrinkled caps,
their bodies smeared with Vaseline. The rest
were there to touch. Strangers, shrunken in trunks,
would push you in, splash you, hold you under
until you nearly drowned — just wholesome fun.
Swimmers, whose only small talk's sadists' tales
of cocks sucked down the deep end's outlet hole,
(their owners had the choice — lose it or drown)
and razors stuck in water-chutes that carved
girl divers neatly into halves and filled
the pool with blood, staining it for all time,
you'd see them leaving, gripping damp towels,
red-rimmed as syphilitics from the Baths'
cocktail of pee.

My school's pool was politer. We had to
empty our bladders first, (whether we could
or not), and march through anti-verruca stuff.
On Open Days the fathers could be seen
training expensive cine cameras
on older girls emerging from the water,
wet straggles of pubic hair across their thighs,
missing the moment when their scrawnier kids
came first in Crawl. Our aquamarine swim-suits,

old-fashioned but not decent, had hooks and straps
which slipped when water-logged, or came undone
one side, leaving a breast exposed.

Men

I sing of Men — crude, thoughtless, kinky men.

The ones who recommend you to a mate
and bring him round — fat, ugly, hopeful too.
('But why object? He only wants to watch —
well, for the first ten minutes, anyway . . .')

Those who are grieved you're not a lesbian —
they'd bargained on two girls to fill their bed.

The guilty types who ask to be abused —
I'll swear alright, but in my own good time —
or leave, muttering, 'Sorry about last night.'

Each who, unwisely seeks comparisons,
needs constant humouring like a lunatic,
wants A-plus marked in teacher's big black book.

Last, those who in the throes of passion drop
your clothes, then, stop to hang their trousers up.

There's nothing *badly* wrong with blokes like these —
they wouldn't use you as a punching-bag
or ask to have their faces shat upon —
a Civil Service taste I heard from some
Madame's good friend. All that they need to make
them perfect men is some *good* woman's love.
I'm glad that I am not that sort.

Paying For Sex

A Hollywood actress who'd come to stay
with a born-again film extra in Richmond
asked where she could pay for sex in London.
On being told that there was no such place,
she asked, 'How do you manage then?'

The answer is — we manage badly.
Free sex is something like the NHS —
months to get down to it with some coy types.
And all the details that you have to tell!
The form my mother filled for glasses
was no worse.

First, there's the questionnaire to place your class —
on education, work and cash. (They're pleased
if you earn *slightly* less than them — enough
to dress well, pay your way, but not enough
to make them feel inferior.) Next comes
the one on sex — how many men you've had,
what did you do with or to whom. And all
to see if you are worthy of a fuck.

Men who'd buy endless rounds when with the boys
mentally price us up as — two lagers
or six gins — turn surly if they've got it wrong.
(A whole distillery would be too low
a price for some of them; and yet, if we
are simply generous, we're labelled 'cheap'.)
I think we're less inclined to price, although I've heard
some careful girls get night-attire from Marks
then take it back if the seduction fails,
ensuring they don't waste more than they paid
for Durex planted in their flatmate's drawers
to be discovered in all innocence.

And there are men who dub you 'beautiful',
who also need 'I love you's' said before.
Romantic shits – they're first to knock you off
the pedestal they put you on. Goddess
becomes Aunt Sally, crown – a dunce's cap,
when all is done.

That actress wished to pay a straighter price –
to keep control and honestly enjoy
it like an evening at the theatre,
where players, who are good and love their job,
stand up to do their bit. I see her point.
Yet, all that is conventional in me
shrank back appalled when a man, (pretty
and young as I was), hinted that he'd like
a fiver as 'a souvenir'.

Geography

Each year they passed out Philips' Atlases
full of unmeaning maps I'd try to read –
first the Political – bright pastel rags
of land with river veins – the Physical,
earth colours, yellow, brown and green. I'd scan
the sticky label in the front to see
the book's lineage of fellow-sufferers.
If there were many there, I'd garnish it,
anthropomorphise coastlines – put eyes
in inlets, nostrils in peninsulas.

I used to do my homework lying by
the pale gas fire for warmth. Visitors would
step over me. One trod right on the map
I'd drawn. Miss Foxton, a walking advert
for the role of shoe-adviser, her own
brown leather lace-ups polished like conkers,
thought Africa no place for that grubby
Man-Friday-print and gave me 'E' – a grade
used only for those beyond redemption.

I think I could have liked the subject in
the Middle Ages; but modern textbooks
lack wonder and humanity – précis
of précis, their glossy pages never
show monopods or anthropophagi.
Their servant-teachers are not Mandevilles,
nor like eighteenth century gentlemen,
who, when in Rome, got out their tape measures
to find the truth about St Peter's dome.

Outside school walls, my mind could travel to
Haggard's poetic Zululand, Mark Twain's
fanatically detailed microcosm

of the Mississippi, Verne's islands, ice,
lighthouses and subterraneous wonders.
And I was angered for the dynasty
of navy-ink strangers in my Atlas,
who, in the name of learning, signed to hear
the world chewed up, spat out in terms of tons
of jute, asbestos, cocoa crops and tin.

French Connection

On our way to see French Connection II,
a friend of mine stopped off in Leicester Square
and bought a large vibrator from a shop.
The three of us went in together.
We stood by while the assistant talked
and talked of the advantages of a massage,
and managed in ten minutes not to say
anything dirty – all euphemisms.
Eventually she sold my friend a kind
much larger, dearer and with varied heads,
not only that, but also a long sheath –
bubucled latex, black as liquorice,
warty enough to be the Elephant Man's.
'It's realistic and reduced,' she said.
She put that mandrake in a box full of
neat polystyrene grooves for other bits,
and packaged it in paper – candy-striped.
The cinema was round the corner and
as usual then, the usher searched our bags,
(those were the I R A bomb days). Seeing
the innocent, shoe-box-shaped package there,
he laughed and let it by untouched.

Old Extras

Old extras never die or get the sack,
they simply go on file for horror films –
or so I was told in all seriousness
by a woman on Tale of Two Cities,
part of the Old Bailey mob, or, as one
assistant phrased it, (fearing the Union),
'Gallery personnel'.

As we sat in waist-crushing, hessian skirts,
hair under foul mob-caps, she told us how
she'd been put on that file – 'just by mistake',
and gone to Central Casting, hair fresh-dyed,
proffering new photos, begging 'Take me off.'
It worked. Now she was saving all the cash
for a good face-lift – one thousand pounds.
She looked all right to me, no real wrinkles
at forty odd, the only obvious flaw –
the ripple of a lousy nose-job.

Spells

At twelve or so, we all thought marriage was more
or less compulsory. Half-seriously,
comparing notes with other girls,
I tried old spells – sleeping on wedding-cake,
throwing an apple's peel at Hallowe'en
to form initials and sitting alone
combing my hair out in a darkened room
while I looked for another face in the glass.
I melted lead, too, in the preserving pan,
pouring the molten metal on to water
to find the symbols of *his* profession –
I only got a load of balls.

One of my friends was much more practical,
less of a lover of strange rituals.
She planned to wed a lord, then poison him.
That way she'd skip the sex, but get to keep
the title and the stately home.

Years later, I met her come from Iran.
She'd crossed Afghanistan alone and brought
a souvenir for all the guests to try –
some camel's yoghourt hardened into blocks,
a bit like cakes of paint with hair inside.